I noticed years ago that most people are not anywhere close to where they dream to be in life and that's mainly because they are afraid. Others truly want to live the life of their dreams. They just do not know what to say, what to do, how to do it, or even when to do it.

This book delivers tactical as well as practical information on how to overcome and overachieve at any point in your life. Utilizing the book properly can help virtually anyone create the lifestyle of their choosing all while making their OWN history.

If you are looking for more copies of this book and the *Not Afraid to Be First Workbook* for your team, contact booking@antoniostarr.com to get more information on bulk pricing as well as book customization.

NOT AFRAID TO BE

HOW TO DEVELOP FEARLESS VISION, DISCIPLINE & TRAITS NEEDED TO MAKE YOUR OWN HISTORY

FIRST

Printed in the United States of America

Produced by First Generation Millionaires LLC
Atlanta, Georgia

First Edition 2018

ISBN: 978-1-7324380-0-2 (paperback)
ISBN: 978-1-7324380-2-6 (ebook)
ISBN: 978-1-7324380-1-9 (workbook)

Edited by: Candace Sinclair
Cover and text design by Antonio Starr
www.antoniostarr.com

Dedicated to my pulchritudinous wife Erika and our outstanding children Tatiana and Maceo.

Special thanks to my friend Robyn McComb for helping me put my thoughts together in this book.

LET ME SAY THIS FIRST

Here we are with book number three, and we are talking about not being afraid to be a first. Kinda ironic, huh? One thing I've learned in recent years is that it is truly never too late to do something for the first time.

At the same time, it is also never too early to become a first at something early in life either.

Growing up, I was never first at anything. On second thought, I was pretty much always the one getting in trouble. As a matter of fact, I'm pretty certain I led the line when it was time for some sort of whooping (not whippings or spankings…we got whoopings in the south!) situation at my grandmother's house. Ehhh, it was only right, I guess. I was often the leader of the mischief with my cousins.

Aside from being publicly recognized and rewarded by way of thrashings for my tumultuous ways as a pre-teen, I was pretty much always at the back of the crowd—academics, sports, relationships, you name it. If there was a rating system for it, Antonio was nearly the obscurity mark. It's why and how I developed my impeccable sense of humor and comedic timing (I've read this sentence twenty times and laugh every time, but it's true). I needed a way to stand out in crowds, but it was also my way of overcoming the actual fears I had deep within. I had been in the crowded back for so long that I became comfortable there. The thought of being out front scared the heck out of me, but I had to do it. I had to get uncomfortable with being comfortable if I wanted to be out front where I knew I belonged. I wanted to be first for once.

One thing I know about you is that you have some sort of desire to do something great in your life but will also leave a legacy for your family. Either that or you just like reading the first few pages of random books, or maybe you are my mom who is just proud of her son's accomplishments. Hey, ma! Regardless of your reason for reading this, I want to encourage you to keep going. Keep going through these pages and keep going through your life without fear, family. I feel strongly that within these pages you will find some added fuel to keep your burning desire ablaze.

Being the first at anything in life has never been and will never be easy. You know that, right? The challenges you'll face will make you want to give up daily! There will be times when you will question your decisions and even your sanity, but you can't stop. There will be times in your pursuit of greatness when you will want to settle. Oftentimes in your journey, the voice of your fears will try to reign supreme and attempt to scare you out of your goals. In this book, I along with some other first-time greats will give you the tools you need to combat the fear and overcome your challenges.

Most times there are no precedents to guide someone who has set off on their journey to be FIRST. You may also have little family support, either because your family does not understand what you are doing, or they simply don't possess the resources to support you. You have no clue if you will be successful, and you are probably afraid to strike out and try your luck. Basically, being first means you are alone. No one is there to coddle or guide you. You are probably rather clueless about what to do or how to do it. Being clueless can be completely terrifying. My intention with this book is to be real with you, not to sugarcoat things. Being first is petrifying, but it is more than possible. The end result makes all of the fear, uncertainty, and effort totally worth it! You'll see.

This book will pack a powerful punch. It will make you ask yourself some hard questions, and it will address some of your deepest insecurities. It will force you to take a good long hard look at your life and determine how to change things to bring about the ultimate success you are after. Change is never comfortable, but if you want to become FIRST, change is inevitable. By the end of this book, you will have a clear understanding of what you need to do to become that *first* you desire. Plus, you will have an action plan that will lead you to that success. You will put this book down as a new person, ready to claim your spot out front!

Inside of this book, you will read a lot about fear (if you haven't figured that out already). That is because fear will always be your biggest opposition. The great thing about fear is that it's just energy, and it's all controlled by you. Once you learn how to rechannel that energy…Oh God! You will become an unstoppable force of greatness. Fear is not the only issue holding you back though. What about the negative or stagnant people around you? You will learn how to deal with people like that. What about your lack of skills or education? You will learn how to overcome those hurdles. You will learn about interpersonal relationships. Everything you learn will come from someone else. That means you need to create special relationships that will carry you into success.

You will also gain a lot of information about how to become the kind of person you need to be for success. Becoming FIRST can call for some pretty major personal and lifestyle changes. But if you really want to be first, these changes will be virtually painless and certainly worthwhile. In addition, you will learn all about how to surmount other challenges you may face, such as poor thought habits and negativity. For example, you will learn how to consider nothing a waste and to not let failure hold you back. Why? Because even if you fail, you now have tools and resources to build success off of as you go in another direction. You will also learn how to view challenges as hurdles to jump over rather than road closures that completely obliterate your chances of success. With these mindset shifts, you will become one of the few people in society who continually move forward rather than staying still in life. You may be holding yourself back without realizing it. You may have a bad attitude. You are about to learn the *right* way to think and the *right* way to approach your success.

With the right approach, the right people around you, and a no-fear mindset, you can make your legacy whatever you want it to be. If you don't like the status of your family, you can change that and create a better future for yourself, your future generations, and the family members you have counting on you now. Whether you are a kid still in high school contemplating college or a single parent hoping to provide better for your kids, you can make your own success. You can propel yourself from your current position into your dream position. The power is within you, but you have to do some work to unlock it. This all may seem daunting, but you got this, and I got you!

I'm assuming you also purchased the accompanying *Not Afraid to Be First Workbook* as well. This workbook will be vital in the identification of all your strengths as well as the parts of your life that we need to build up. You will also be able to strategically map out your ACTION plan, which will be vital to your history making. Grab the workbook if you don't have it already.

How did a kid who had to attend summer school in order to graduate high school with a 1.12 GPA go on to become not only the first published author in his family, but also a certified bestselling author? I stopped being afraid to be FIRST! Every skill, trait, maneuver, and discipline displayed in this book I've utilized, and I consistently utilize them in my daily life. They will work for you if you are willing to work for them.

Let's begin.

I want to know about your progress to the front as it enriches me greatly, so before you bury yourself into this content, take a moment to connect with me on the socials:

Facebook: www.facebook.com/antoniostarr

Instagram: www.instagram.com/antoniostarr

Twitter: www.twitter.com/antoniostarr

Email: antonio@antoniostarr.com

OK, are you ready to work for your first-place spot? I knew you would be.

SO WHAT IF YOU DON'T HAVE A FIRST FAMILY

Many people have had their success handed to them. They come from generational wealth, and therefore, the hard work is done for them already. They just walk right into their reserved spot in life, business, and other influential positions. Sure, you may think it is not fair, but life is not fair!

The important thing here is to realize that just because you don't have generational wealth and affluence to stand on does not mean you cannot be FIRST.

When I started writing this book, I spent a lot of time imagining what the cover would look like. One of my ideas was to have silhouettes of people stacked atop each other and then there would be me standing on their proverbial shoulders. This was to symbolize I was standing on the shoulders of my ancestors, but we all do. Whatever our ancestors built before us, it is our job to continue the legacy. I decided against that cover idea, because it has been done before, and I didn't want to confuse the audience as to what this book is about. Truth is, some of us are standing on generations of fortune while the rest of us find ourselves on the crest of generational fear.

The distance between fear and fortune is shortened with information. Most of our ancestors lacked or were never privileged to the information needed to better themselves or their families. Some of our relatives were so intimidated by the powers that be that they resorted to playing it safe in lieu of causing problems for their existing and future generations. So now we are wedged in these generational cycles of constant lack, or constant growth, but every cycle can be broken and improved. One thing to keep in mind is for the most part, no one can show you any more than they have been shown, so we mustn't be upset with our ancestors if we are from the cycle of lack. Me personally, I rest in the thought that my ancestors did what they thought was best to survive.

One thing I know for sure is that regardless of your family's background, you can make your life whatever you want it to be. You do not have to settle for or be defined by your family legacy if you choose not to be. You can take your lineage from the back to FIRST! You are stronger than you realize. Your ancestors have shown you how to survive without much, so now you can survive the challenges associated with making your family a FIRST family. The information is in your hands right now. It's time to manifest.

Your Belief System

The way you look at life and the attitude you have towards life's possibilities can really influence how you approach achieving success. It is critical to change your attitude to make good lifestyle changes and become FIRST. In the context of this section, your attitude is your belief system. Meaning how strongly you believe in you and your ability to accomplish things in spite of your circumstances. The more you truly believe in your abilities, the more you're likely to conquer in life. That family history we talked about along with your current environment tends to play a big role in your level of belief, but you're ultimately in control of this mindset.

A lot of people have found themselves in the position where their belief system has been beaten out of them over time, so they tend to naturally respond to new opportunities with "I can't..." and then fill in the blank with some excuse. This is what you call a limited belief system. You've placed limits on your imagination, your self expectations and your desire for more.

How often do you think thoughts like:

I can't afford that.

I can't make time for that.

I can't do that because I don't know how...

I can't because I'm too old/young.

I can't change who I am.

I can't go to school because...

Some other similar thought that starts with "I can't..."

It is time to have a different approach. Instead of thinking, "I can't..." start thinking, "How can I...?" Start thinking about *how* to achieve things. This makes things seem possible to you. You are then faced with finding out how to do something, which leads you to creating a plan and taking action.

"If my mind can conceive it, and my heart can <u>believe it</u>, then I can achieve it."

—Muhammad Ali

We're going to build your belief system through the roof in this book. You're going to learn how to trick your mind into believing anything is possible. Because it is!

Leave Your Comfort Zone

Your comfort zone is what you know in life. It is not necessarily a good thing, but you are used to it, so it feels better than taking a gamble and trying something new. Here's the problem with the comfort zone: It encourages you to stay static. To become FIRST, you must change pretty much everything about yourself, but you don't want to do this if you are stuck in your comfort zone. Your subconscious mind has been programmed to like comfort and it asks, "Why should I change? I'm comfortable where I'm at. I'm surviving. Why change?" Say hello to one of your biggest opponents—your subconscious mind. Forcing yourself out of your comfort zone forces your subconscious to reprogram itself. If you never get comfortable in any position in life, your subconscious mind will never get comfortable. It will always want more for you.

Your family can also really make you feel stuck. After all, this is the life you are used to because it was how you were raised. You don't know anything else. Obviously, you can survive following the lifestyle that you have been living your whole lifetime. Here's the thing, from now on, I want you to remove the word *survive* from your vocabulary. From this day forward, your focus is to thrive in life. You will teach all the survivors in your family how to become thrivers for their family.

The comfort zone represents stasis and stagnation. There is no advancement in life when you do the same things, hang out with the same people, and stay complacent with what you currently have. You have to drop this idea that you need to stay in the comfort zone. Instead, you want to branch out and do new things. You even need to do things that scare you sometimes. Only when you start to do new things will you see new changes in your life.

How can you change your comfort zone?

Go out and talk to new people.

Take a class to gain a new skill.

Apply for a job that you don't think you can get.

Change jobs or even careers.

Change who you hang out with.

Move to a new place, new area, or to another country.

Go back to school, no matter how smart or how challenged you think you are.

Approach and talk to a new stranger every day.

Go to a new place to hang out.

Take on a new hobby.

Try working on a new project.

Attend a business networking event.

Approach investors with your invention or business plan.

Talk to the bank about a business loan.

Host fundraisers to raise money for your dream.

The Resistance

To change something in your life, you will encounter resistance. What are some types of resistance you may face?

Unsupportive family and/or friends.

People who say you can't do it.

People who encourage you to stay in your current lifestyle.

Monumental lifestyle overhauls that feel too hard for you to handle.

Lack of finances for education or business capital.

Fear.

Limiting beliefs.

Not knowing where to begin.

Running into new money problems.

Resistance happens. The forces that hold you in your current lifestyle are pretty powerful. However, these forces are more than possible to overcome. You have to think, "This is a challenge to overcome" instead of "I give up! This is too hard! Why is life so hard?" When you think, "Is this worth all the trouble?" consider how you will miss out on your dream if you give up. Yes, it's definitely worth it!

One of the most critical things you need to do to become FIRST is to find motivation. What is motivation? Motivation is something that gives you the will to press forward despite obstacles. It makes you want to reach your goals and achieve your dreams. Even when you are discouraged or facing gut-wrenching challenges, motivation drives you to keep moving forward. I've found that those who have tied their motivation to another person or a purpose tend to have a lot more fight in them. Who or what are you doing this for?

You can draw motivation from many different sources. One being this book, but your vision should be one of your biggest motivating factors. We will talk about how to cast a solid and clear vision for yourself later in the book. You can also pull motivation from the people in your life, which is why it will be very important to surround yourself with motivated individuals. Trust me, you will need to borrow a lot of motivation on this journey to be FIRST. Of course, I will walk you through the process of team building in later chapters.

HOMEWORK TIME!

Refer to your *Not Afraid to Be First Workbook* to complete the **Chapter 1 exercise**.

DON'T SET YOUR GOALS, SET YOUR DREAMS

Everyone talks about setting goals. Don't get me wrong, goals are a good thing. They point you in the right direction, but goals are just simple, one-time tasks that you must complete to reach your dreams. Setting your dreams is far more powerful. Dreams are what you live for.

When you think about them, they paint a smile on your face. They are your reason to try, to love, to live, to soar. Dreams give you wings and make anything seem possible. Your heart skips a beat when your true dream plays in your head. Doesn't it?

So right now, you need to focus on setting your dreams rather than goals. Goals come next as part of your action plan to achieve a dream. While you set your dreams, dream big. Nothing is too impossible or too good for you! Dare to think outside the box and come up with your deepest desires. These are now the things you are going to work on achieving.

Tattoo It on Your Brain!

Right now, you have one big dream to become FIRST. That is a great start. But you need to go deeper than that. What will you be the first in your family to do? What do you want to accomplish? What do you want to become known for? As a kid, what did you dream of becoming, and why did you let that dream go?

Your dream can't just be some vague fantasy about being the first in your family to do *blank*. No! It needs to be something specific, something real, something tangible. Your dream can be to become the first in your family to go to college, or the first to travel outside of your home country, or the first to start a business. Your dream can be to get into politics and change the world, or it can be to do charity work overseas, or it can be to join the military. Your dream can even be something like moving out of the neighborhood where you grew up. Maybe you want to start your own family somewhere that's better, safer, and more established.

Your dream can be anything. But it needs to be something concrete that you can actually visualize. Only then can you start working on this dream.

If your dream is vague, you won't have the first idea how to start working on it. But when it is set in concrete, you can start making lists and taking steps to achieve your dream. Your dream is a big, clear target that you are aiming to hit. It will guide you, direct you, push you, and help you shape your life into what it needs to be in order for you to become FIRST.

What Kind of History Do You Want to Make?

The people you read about in your history books were once just unknown ordinary people. Then they did something that made others notice them. It was big news. Now everyone knows who they are. By becoming FIRST, you actually are making history. You are becoming a key figure in the evolution of your family. You are setting an example for others to follow. Above that, you are proving to yourself what you are capable of.

This is a big deal!

Don't underestimate how big of a deal your desire to become FIRST is. You really are making a huge difference—in your life, in your family, and in society. What kind of legacy do you want to leave for future generations? What do you want to become known for, both in your family tree and in society as a whole? How do you want to introduce yourself, and what do you want your story to look like?

Ask yourself these questions and imagine the future when you make it and accomplish whatever dream you hold near and dear to your heart. You want to create a history you can be proud of, right? So imagine what would make you proud and how it would look. Now tattoo that on your brain!

Dare to Dream Big

So many people are scared to dream big. We talk more about fear in the next chapter, but for now, you need to set fear aside. Let your imagination run wild for a second. You can dream big. Dream HUGE! Dream whatever you want to dream and don't you dare think, "I can't." Think about what you really want to do. What would feed your soul and make you happy? What would make you enjoy life while bettering your current situation?

Also, think posterity. How will your dream affect future generations? You are creating a legacy so make it a good one. Create a dream that will make a lasting positive impact on future generations. Think about what you wish you had in your life growing up. Then consider creating that for yourself as well as other people. Perhaps you wish you had more guidance in school, so consider providing that guidance to other kids. Or maybe you wished that you had some sort of program to help you finance college or a start-up business. Now you can focus on creating such a program for the world. These are just examples. You should listen to your own heart and find what you want to do to shape your own dream.

It is OK to keep your dreams private. People can be really, really negative. Telling people about your dreams is a great way to get negative feedback and discouragement from people. Consider keeping your dreams under wraps to avoid discouragement and judgment, but if you've already tattooed your dream on your brain, then let it all hang out, family. Forget those negative folks!

Plant Your Seed

To grow a dream, you must first plant your dream seed. This process is just as you may be imagining right now. Instead of planting a seed into the earth, you are planting your seed into the universe. Writing your dream down is *the* first step in the process. When you write it down, you are committing to it. The planting process is scary, because you can't physically see your dream grow, but you must remain committed to the growth process. You must allow your dream seed to take root and germinate under what may appear as adversity and pain aka the storms, but you must know that all seeds need sunshine and rain to grow. Once it takes root, you must keep watering it with actions to make it flourish into a full-fledged blossoming and fruitful plant. That plant is a metaphor for your dream in action, as it starts to give you what you want in life and weathers the storms that life can send your way. Your dreams will grow to be your protection.

One thing you can do is create a dream board. Take a piece of cardboard and tape extremely visual pictures to it that represent your dream. You can even get creative by using puffy paint, markers, or whatever you want to make the board seem exciting and inspiring. Then hang it up somewhere so you can see it and touch it often. This keeps your dreams on your mind and insures they remain worthwhile to you. Having dreams on paper also makes them seem more achievable. It's a little trick for the subconscious mind that actually works, so try it out.

Set Goals

So now that you have set your dream, it is time for the next step. This step is really fun because it basically leads you to action. This step is where you set the goals that make your dreams come true.

Here are several examples of good goals:

Enroll in college. Attend classes, do your homework, and get good grades so you can graduate.

Get fit enough to be admitted into the military and complete basic training.

Get healthy enough to lead the life of your dreams. This goal can be broken into smaller steps, such as losing weight or learning how to manage stress better.

Get funding for a business and draw up an actionable business plan to present to investors or loan givers.

Move out of your current area into a better living situation.

Find a partner to help you in business.

Publish your book.

Develop an app and get it published.

Find a way to manufacture your invention so you can present investors with something concrete.

Get your GED if you didn't graduate high school. That way, you can go to college.

These are just a few examples of goals you can set, but your goals will depend on your situation and your dream. To determine the goals you need to set, you really need to list everything you want. Then list everything you don't currently have. Make goals centered around obtaining the things you need in order to make your dreams come true.

There Is No Time to Waste

It has been said throughout the generations that good things come to those who wait. I don't know who invented that saying because waiting for life to hand you things just does not work. You know that firsthand by this point. Instead of waiting around for your goals to just happen and your dreams to just manifest, you need to take some action to make them happen. Therefore, list the actions you can take to accomplish your dream, then take them. This is the only way to make your dreams come true. You have to use some elbow grease!

When you start listing goals, you begin to feel empowered. Suddenly, your dream is more possible because it is a simple list of tasks to undertake. Each task you accomplish is one step closer to your dream's full actualization. Your goals can be broken into sub-goals. Undertake each sub-goal to reach your main goal. Set one major goal that will help you accomplish your dream. Then break that into sub-goals. Sub-goals are the little steps you need to take to make your big goal, and eventually your dream come true. For example, if you want to open your own restaurant, you need to create a series of sub-goals for procuring funding, drafting a business plan, finding a great location, marketing, etc.

Celebrate Each Victory

"Life is what happens while you're making plans," is a great John Lennon quote that sums this principle up. While you are working on your dream, realize that life is still happening. To live the dream, you need to learn to appreciate life and enjoy yourself along the way. Otherwise, you will become miserable and your dream will start to feel like work, and we know what happens when it starts to feel like work. We quit! So when you accomplish a goal on your list and slide one step closer to your main goal, you need to take a moment to celebrate. Reward yourself for your hard work. Enjoy the victory and the glory of accomplishing what you set out to do.

Do you even realize what you are accomplishing right now? You are doing something monumental and hugo for yourself, for your family, and for everyone in the world! You are setting an example and proving to yourself (the most important person) that you really can improve your life if you just work at it.

One thing you cannot do is get caught up in the celebration to the point you forget there is still more work to do. I've seen people hit a few goals and think they've made it big time. With that attitude, they celebrate so hard and so long that they end up putting themselves further away from their ultimate goal.

Stay focused.
Stay disciplined,
but also, stay having fun!

HOMEWORK TIME!

Refer to your *Not Afraid to Be First Workbook* to complete the Chapter 2 exercise.

OVERCOMING THE FEAR THAT HOLDS YOU BACK

As human beings, we are often fearful of the unknown. Fearful of loss, of rejection, of failure; but when you entertain that fear, you let it take root in your heart and then you let it hold you back. It's time to overcome the fear because it's not real anyway!

In 2013, Will Smith starred in a movie that he himself called "the most painful failure" of his career. The movie was called *After Earth*, and I have to agree with Will that it was quite painful to watch, but there was a very powerful moment in that movie.

(I did sit through the entire painstaking process of watching it). There was a scene where he had to send his son on a solo mission armed with not much more than one of those cool flying suits. His son was noticeably afraid to be out in the unknown by himself, so to calm him and his fears, Smith delivered these powerful words:

"Fear is not real. It is a product of thoughts you create. Do not misunderstand me, danger is very real, but fear is a choice."

Powerful!

Be Stronger than Your Fears

Ultimately, fear will rise up within you. From there, it's up to you what you do with it. You can decide to let it take control, or you can decide to overcome it and banish it. If you want to become FIRST, you MUST do the latter. You have to be stronger than your fear!

Call it anxiety, worry, nerves, terror, whatever you want—it's still fear. It's that numbing, paralyzing feeling in your gut. It's that thought that makes you want to turn around in your tracks and give up for good.

Everything you think and do can either nurture or kill that seed you've planting within yourself. Everyone gets scared, family. Some of your greatest idols (idolize no one) are terrified about something on a daily basis, but they've learned to overcome that fear.

Like the late great Michael Jackson once said in his hit, "Wanna Be Starting Something:" 'Too high to get over, (yeah yeah). Too low to get under (yeah yeah). You're stuck in the middle (yeah yeah) and the pain is thunder.'" That's how fear makes you feel family, so you have to make up your mind to either go around it or plow straight through it. Just make up your mind to get past it. A made-up mind is a heck of a fertilizer. #Marinate

Fear kills more dreams than failure ever will. Fear is the antithesis to dreams. Fears are basically nightmares. We all know that nightmares are dreadful. But do nightmares kill you? No! I grew up in the era of Freddy Krueger (some of you may have to Google that guy's name). Freddy had us terrified to go to sleep, because we thought he would actually come and kill us in our dreams. Seriously! Soon, we realized just as Will Smith's character did in that movie that neither Freddy nor our fears were real, and thus, we were no longer frightened. So just as we overcame those nightmares, we overcame our fears as well, and so can you. No matter how unpleasant they are.

Do you have affirmation statements in your daily routine? If not, you should get yourself some ASAP! (I have a feeling this will come up in the homework section.). I speak my affirmations out loud daily. Multiple times a day even.

"I am a magnet for success and good fortune. Great people and great opportunities are attracted to me."

"I am an attractor of positivity and a detractor of negative people and their energy without even trying."

"My vision will be bigger than my fear today because people are counting on me."

These are just a few of my affirmations that you are more than welcomed to borrow and modify as you see fit. There is something about speaking your affirmations aloud daily that causes your subconscious mind to reprogram itself. You do know that you can trick your subconscious mind (where fear comes from) to believe anything you tell it right? Try it.

OK, family, I've given you examples from Will Smith to Freddy Krueger to Michael Jackson and now affirmations. I've tried to show you in several different ways that the number one thing that holds most of us back is all make believe. I sure hope I've gotten you through that one thing that appeared to be too high to get over and too low to get under at one point. We have things to do, so let's keep pushing forward.

BUT! Before we move on in the book, let's look at some lies you may still be telling yourself out of fear. As you go through these ridiculously outlandish thoughts, I want you to see how silly they sound when reading them.

You: There is no chance I can succeed when my family hasn't.

Me: Get out of here with that crazy talk! No one said being FIRST was going to be easy. You must not allow another generation of your family to die off without trying based on something your ancestors did or did not do. It starts with you. Say that aloud right now. *"IT STARTS WITH ME!"*

You: I might spend a lot of money and not make any in return.

Me: Money comes and goes family. Money invested in a dream (you invest in your dreams) is always money well spent. Even if you lose some money working on a dream, you should always look for the valuable lessons that are returned as a result. Not all returns will be financial, but it's the lessons that will prove more valuable in the long run. Trying asking yourself, "How much will I lose in life if I do not go for it?"

You: People might judge me.

Me: Well, who cares what other people think? This is your life! People will be negative and even jealous that you are striking out and trying to become first. As mentioned earlier, some of these people are just trying to cast their fears onto you. By the way, you will always be judged. Would you rather be judged for doing nothing or judged for being great?

You: I may get rejected.

Me: Yes, and you may get accepted. The only rejection that can ever stop you is the rejection from yourself. Not trying should scare the heck out of you if you're afraid of rejection. Consider what might happen if you actually succeed. Give yourself a chance. You won't know until you try, right? Don't leave yourself stuck in the middle. The pain is thunder. Did you know that JK Rowling was rejected over a hundred times before publishing her famous Harry Potter series and now she is richer than the Queen of England? Imagine that.

You: I am not that smart.

Me: I graduated high school at the bottom of my class, but I went on to build a corporate career where I managed multi-million-dollar budgets; and I had a staff of direct reports who were all college graduates. So what if you're not smart? I'm not smart either. Just be determined and always willing to learn new things. This way you will develop your intelligence. Intelligent people run the world. The smart people work for them.

Commitment

Once upon a time, I was talking with my wife in our master bathroom, and she mentioned how nice it would be to have a small television installed in the wall. This was long before flat screen TV's were around, or shall I say affordable for the common man, so we still had the old school tube televisions. Anyway, my wife was talking about how she could catch up on the news and see the weather and traffic report as she got ready for work.

I asked her where she wanted the television located and she pointed out the spot. I left the bathroom for a brief moment, returned with a huge ball-peen hammer and then…Bam! I knocked a huge hole in the wall where she wanted the television installed. She looked at me in shock and said, "What was that?!?!?" to which I replied, "That's my commitment hole. Now I have to install this TV."

This is the attitude you must have when it comes to committing to your dreams and goals, family. If you are serious about becoming FIRST, then you need to make a commitment hole, cut, investment, or something right now. Even if you haven't completed your list or any of the tasks in the previous chapters, you have to show your commitment to your ultimate dream immediately.

Are you ready for that?

What did you do to show your commitment just now?

Write it down in the space below.

It's hard to turn back on a dream once you have made solid commitments to bring it into fruition. Do something you can't turn back from. Do something that forces you to complete a project, or else a big hole will be left behind.

Intuition

It's important to listen to your intuition, aka your gut. I tell people all the time, "God is in your gut." If your gut is telling you to go for it then allow nobody to convince you otherwise. This is your dream. I honestly feel like God is giving me the confirmation that I'm on the right path when I feel it in my gut.

Following your intuition takes a tremendous amount of courage because, well, we are not perfect, and honestly, sometimes things may go wrong. That doesn't mean your intuition was necessarily wrong though. In these trying times, you more than likely will hear from the "I told you so" crowd, but you must stay committed. Some people will have very convincing arguments to get you to doubt yourself, but you can never allow their outer voices to be louder than your inner voice.

Don't Get Stuck on What Others Think

People will always have their own opinions about you and the moves you make. Are their opinions always right? Absolutely not! Do their opinions pay the bills? Heck no! Do they live life in your shoes? No! When I have people come to me to express their frustrations about others and their opinions of them, I ask this one simple question, "Would you switch your life with that person?" Nine times out of ten, they say, "No!"

So remember this: if you would not switch lives with the person who has an opinion about you, then why would you even entertain what they have to say? You're just as insane as they are if you let them control your moves.

Be Audacious

"Can you believe she did that?"

"Yeah, she must have a lot of nerve!"

Imagine how miffed people might be when you go against their limiting advice or discouragement and do what you want instead. Imagine how hot they will be as you actually succeed and become FIRST. They will call you bougie, high and mighty, and any number of other bad things, but guess what? You did it and they didn't. Their irritation is simply jealousy.

So have the audacity to go after your dreams, no matter what others tell you or what others think. Have the audacity to ignore those who tell you no and try to make you fail. Have the audacity to defy the odds and make society reel back in shock. Have the audacity to laugh at your fears and break through them. Have the audacity not to prove your naysayers wrong, but to prove yourself right!

Pioneer

You are a pioneer right now, the first to cross America in a covered wagon, the first to drift out into space. You are going into unexplored territory, with no one to lead you. You don't know what to expect or what will happen. At the end, though, you may discover gold (metaphorically or literally), or make an amazing scientific breakthrough. Your success will lead to a significant change in the world. You have to believe that.

So even if you are terrified, just think back to the first man in space or the first pioneers to cross the Old West. They were scared yet they made amazing discoveries. You are scared but you may just make an amazing discovery too.

Just the thought of being first at anything is exciting to me, and to be the first person in my family to be the example for all others to follow is just mind-blowing. Just think about the stories your future generations will tell about you. When they mention your name, they will have to add in that you were the First Generation to succeed at something. First Generation Doctor, First Generation Military Officer, First Generation Millionaire, First Whatever! I like the sound of that. I bet you do too.

Throw Your Entire Self into It

I loved having conversations with my late grandmother back in the days. She was not well educated, but oh so wise. She was a God-fearing woman who read her Bible religiously. Somewhere in our talks, she'd drop her mandatory quote from her good book. One of those quotes she hit me with is one I will share with you now.

"Blessed are those who believe without seeing."

— John 20:29

In the context of our discussion, my grandmother was talking about believing in God without actually seeing him; but in this book's context, I am talking about believing in your end result before you can physically see it. Most people have to see it to believe it, but since we've already established you are not most people, you must believe to see it. Once you can vividly see your end result, you can then allow yourself to fully commit to the process of manifesting that vision. When I say fully commit to the process, I mean throwing your entire self into it— mind, body, spirit, blood, sweat, tears, dedication, determination, all of that.

No fear!

The Problem with Fear Projecting

How much of your fear has been planted in your heart by someone else?

You may have someone who projects his or her fears onto you to protect you. For example, your mother may say, "What if you fail?" because she doesn't want to see you hurt. Your spouse may say, "How could you drop out of school to start a business? You're throwing your life away!" But you can't let these fears make you scared to move forward.

You may also be around toxic people who can't stand to see you succeed. They try to poison you with fear and doubt so you don't even try and thus don't stand a chance. You can recognize these people because they are never happy or excited for you when you do something great. They always have something negative to say. I bet you can think of a few of these people right now. Some of them you call friends, and as the great poet Ecstasy from the famed rap group Whodini once said, "…with friends like that you don't need enemies." We will discuss these friends, family, and haters more in depth a little later in the book.

Whether they are doing it out of love or hate, it all has the same result on your psyche if you allow them to project their fears on you.

Resist!

Fear is Growth

When you first rode a bike without training wheels, how did you feel? When you first dove off the high board, how did you feel? When you first asked your crush out, how did you feel? I bet you were scared. I bet your heart was beating in your throat. I bet your palms were sweaty and your knees were knocking. But because of that fear, you grew and learned something that you know like the back of your hand now.

Believe it or not, when you are scared, you are growing. Fear is a symptom of when you venture out of your comfort zone and take steps toward your dream's actualization. You are the pioneer, remember this. You won't grow without encountering some scary stuff.

Take Advantage of Opportunities

When Oprah Winfrey moved from rural Mississippi to Baltimore to work in TV, she had no clue what would happen. She didn't know if she was going to make it or if she was going to hate Baltimore. Then she was recruited by a Chicago TV station to host a morning show. Again, she had no clue if she was going to thrive in Chicago, or if she might be fired within one week. Yet she took the leap anyway and ended up becoming the household name we all know now. Oprah took advantage of an opportunity, and it led her to stardom.

An opportunity almost always comes with a leap. You might have to move for a new job. You will make more money, but you are not sure if you will love or hate where you relocate to. Or you may have to spend a little money to start a business, and you have no idea if that business will actually take off and pay back your investment. Opportunity is great…until you realize you have to risk something and take a leap of faith to see if the reward even comes. If you don't take that leap, you will never know what may have happened.

Start saying "Absolutely" instead of "No, I shouldn't because what if…?" or "No, I can't because… (insert excuse)." Remember your affirmation statements.

Embrace a New Environment

When I was in the sixth grade, my father decided to join the Army. After basic training, his first duty station was in Colorado Springs, Colorado. Fort Carson to be exact. There I was, this impressionable black kid from a small segregated town in Southwest Georgia (Blakely, Georgia, to be exact) on his way out west. Up until our moving day, all I really knew was what I had learned from the people in my neighborhood. I didn't really hang out with anyone that didn't look like me.

Once we arrived and got settled in our new home thousands of miles from my comfort zone, it was all weird for me. There were so many different looking people in Colorado. They spoke different languages and ate different foods than what the white and black people in my hometown ate. It didn't take me long to adjust to this new environment. Actually, I fell in love with this new environment rather quickly. In all honesty, it was that time in my life that changed me forever. I learned there is so much more to life than the environment we grow up in. The more you are exposed to other environments, the wealthier you can become. I can now embed myself into virtually any environment and thrive, and it's all because I was forced out of my environment.

Change your environment and watch your life change. Embrace new environments as a sign that your life is changing because it is.

Do Something Every Day That Scares You

"Do something every day that scares you." This quote by Eleanor Roosevelt should be everyone's motto in life. Why? Because it perfectly represents how going out of your comfort zone can be terrifying, yet so rewarding. When you do something every day that scares you, you learn new things. You find out that fears you have are not real. You teach yourself to overcome fear and live life to the fullest.

In your venture to become FIRST, start trying to live this way. The fear you feel is a good sign that you are making some changes and embarking on a magnificent journey into a changed life. Let your fear turn into adrenalin that excites you.

HOMEWORK TIME!

Refer to your *Not Afraid to Be First Workbook* to complete the Chapter 3 exercise.

GO BEYOND YOUR CAPACITY

On May 2, 1953, an athlete named Sir Roger Bannister set out to do something that no man had ever done. He wanted to be the FIRST person to run a sub four-minute mile. This means he challenged himself to race a full mile in less than four minutes.

After a valiant effort, Bannister's time in that race at Oxford was 4:03.6, which is phenomenal, but still short of his goal. Roger Bannister knew that in order for him to be the first to accomplish this goal, he had to go well beyond his current capacity, and he wasn't afraid to do just that.

Following another failed attempt on June 7 of that same year (4:02.0), Bannister went into heavy training mode to stretch himself and his capacity both mentally and physically.

It was on May 4, 1954 that Bannister once again set out to manifest his dreams. Not a single person outside of Bannister and his team thought a sub four-minute mile was possible. As a matter of fact, the "experts" of the sport were 100 percent sure that no man could break four minutes. Does that sound familiar to you? All the experts who have never accomplished what you are determined to accomplish casting their opinions, or shall I say *fears* on you? Keep reading.

With the assistance of his team (more on them later), Roger Bannister gave absolutely all he had inside him in that race and finished with a time of…three minutes and 59.4 seconds! He'd done it. He proved to himself what he could do despite what history, family, friends, or those so-called experts had to say. But you want to know what was more inspiring than Roger Bannister being a FIRST? It was the fact that forty-six days later a runner by the name of John Landy beat Bannister's record time with a three-minute 57.9 mile. Do you see what happened there? By Roger Bannister not being afraid to be first, he not only increased his belief and capacity, but he increased the belief and capacity of others as well.

Since May 4, 1954, tons of runners have been clocked under four minutes for a mile run, and here is the kicker—the sub four-minute mile is now the standard for top athletes. This is how you making a decision to go beyond your capacity can cause a ripple in civilization as we know it. Don't take your dreams for granted family. You can create a new standard of greatness.

I say this so you will know you can't expect to succeed if you don't push yourself. You have to leave your comfort zone and embrace things you did not imagine possible before. In other words, go beyond your capacity, and you will find that your capacity increases. Believe it or not, you can surprise yourself! You are more able and capable than you think you are right now.

While writing this book, Sir Roger Bannister passed away. Rest In Peace, history maker

Beat Social Conditioning

(Morpheus voice) What if I told you that you have been conditioned by society?

Well, the bad news is you have been conditioned. You have been made to believe you are not capable of great things. The good news is all of that conditioning is hogwash. You can banish it from your head and stop letting it drag you down. Here's another affirmation statement that just came from God:

"I will banish my conditioning like Bannister!"

That may sound a little corny, but it's true. You must master the art of banishing all that society has conditioned you to believe that is counterproductive to you winning your own race.

If you grew up poor, as a minority, or as a "blue collar" worker, you may have been fed a certain mindset. The rest of society, including your own family, probably believes there is no point trying to be greater, because what you have right now is all you will ever have.

That's a bunch of bull!

You also must be aware of your own complacency. Complacent people are not successful because they have no desire to change. Roger Bannister set a goal to be the first person to run a sub four-minute mile. Imagine if he would have settled for that 4:02 mile on his second attempt? How would that have impacted the world? When you set your goal, and you throw your entire self into making it happen, then you must settle for nothing less. Complacency reduces your capacity, and we are all about going beyond our capacity right now. Stretch!

When you start to feel that you can't do something, or when someone says you can't, remember, this is just how most of us have been conditioned to think. By changing your attitude and challenging the concepts that have been planted in your head, you can make some amazing progress.

Practice

What are you good at? I bet you weren't always good at that one thing. You probably sucked when you first tried. Your handwriting was atrocious in kindergarten (mine is still atrocious); you fell on your butt when you first roller skated; you couldn't make a shot to save your life when you first started playing basketball, but you practiced and as a result, you became stellar at something. You can't expect yourself to succeed the first time you try. If you want to become good at something, then you have to practice.

How many hours do you think Sir Bannister had to practice before he accomplished his goal? How many times do you think he failed while practicing? I'm sure it was dozens if not hundreds of times, but within each failure is a lesson as long as you get back up and keep trying. There is a saying, "Practice makes perfect," but I disagree with that mantra. Perfect practice makes perfect, family. Practice is the place where you perfect your technique. Practice is the place where you identify your weaknesses. Practice is the place where you can get help to turn your weaknesses into strength. Practice is the place where you can get it wrong several times, and there is no one there to bash or discourage you. The more you practice, the better you will perform when people are watching. #Marinate

If you want to be a top runner yourself, then you should practice running every day! Want to be the next tech guru? Well, you better have some technology in your hand for nearlyevery waking hour practicing your craft. Right now, someone is out there with the same goal as you who is practicing while you are still a victim of complacency and fear. It's time to go to work. Excuse me, it's time to go to practice!

Be Creative

The most successful people in the world started out with just a seed of an idea. That idea was different, unique, weird even. Back in the 80s, did people know what Windows was? No! But Bill Gates created Windows, and now it's a standard operating system. Just twenty years ago, did people think you could use computers to order food and chat with friends on Facebook? No, but now it's a big thing because various entrepreneurs got creative with how to use what was previously just a government communication tool, now known as the Internet. Everything you have today started out as some creative idea. Every business was just a shot in the dark at first made by one bold person.

Don't just do what has been done before, or you will get swallowed up in the oversaturated market. There are a lot of other fish in the sea, and they are all trying to make money. You are not unique in that sense. To truly become successful, you have to stand out from the crowd so you actually attract attention and make a difference.

You also need to be creative to surmount your challenges. You have to think of ways to defy the odds and make your dreams happen, regardless of the struggles mounted against you. Say you can't afford college to get your dream career. Think of ways to get that career and relative work experience without college or find ways to pay for college.

One thing that really embodies creativity is figuring out how to use your background to give you a leg up. You could win a scholarship by writing an inspiring essay about your background and your vision to help future generations by setting a great example of how anyone can be FIRST. Or you can use your story to help you earn empathy from clients and get better sales. Use what you have to make something amazing. Remember, you don't have to be "smart" or carry a degree to be creative. Honestly, most forward-thinking people in power tend to gravitate more towards creatives than the decorated anyway.

Resist the Devil

This section may offend some people, but I have to give you my truth. I think the character that is the devil is one of the most successful creations ever. Growing up in my household with my grandmother that I mentioned earlier in the book was a very interesting one. Mainly because we spent a lot of time in church, and it seemed like the devil was a bigger topic than God was in most sermons. I honestly think the best way for others to inject fear in us is to use the devil's name as the needle.

I watched so many people give up on their dreams when one thing went wrong. It was because they thought the devil tried to stop them. It was and still is sad to watch people defeat themselves all in the name of the devil. We've been programmed to believe that everything that goes wrong is the devil, and everything that goes right is because of God. I don't subscribe to that at all. I believe wholeheartedly that God sometimes tests our faith in ourselves and our vision just to see how bad we want it. These tests, when successfully passed, build up our resistance of the devil even more.

I believe the devil is more fear, discouragement, despair, laziness, uncertainty, complacency, and like emotions than he is a person. These emotions make you want to just give up. You have to resist this pull and not let the devil aka fear influence your decisions.

When you come face to face with the devil, which will happen many times on your journey to become FIRST, you gotta crush the emotions that are hampering your success. Literally crush them!

The best way to do this is to chase each negative emotion away with a positive one. You feel fear? Force yourself to feel hope. You feel discouraged? Use your affirmation statements to build yourself back up. Feeling complacent? Go back to your goals and see where you are in relation to where you said you will be. One thing they used to say in church that I agree with is, *"The devil will not win!"* Your fears cannot and will not win. You will win!

Fight for What is Right

How hot do you get when something unjust or unfair happens to you? You get really hot, right? That heat you feel, that burning drive, is *passion*. And passion drives you to speak up, to take action, to do something about it! If you fight for what is right, you are running off of pure, unfiltered passion. And what a rush that is.

Standing up for yourself and what you think is right makes some sort of difference. Even if you don't think your voice will matter, speaking up for the minority makes sure that the minority is at least heard.

Some of the biggest social justice warriors are now household names. They really made a difference in driving social change, even though the odds and all of society were stacked overwhelmingly against them. Think Rosa Parks and Martin Luther King, Jr. They made a difference by speaking up and so can you.

You may not have aspirations of being a social injustice warrior but standing up for your dreams requires the same passion. Regardless of what you are going to accomplish in your life, you have to remember you are doing this for something way greater than yourself. That's not pressure, that's passion.

Find What You Can Do Differently

If what you've done in the past is failing to produce the results you desire, then it's possible something needs to change. Review what you are doing and question why it is not working. Then think of ways you can do things differently to bring about success. In a later chapter, I'll introduce you to this guy named Eddie the Eagle. Eddie the Eagle competed and made history in the Olympics back in the 80s as a ski jumper; but before that, he attempted (feebly at that) to become a downhill skier at which he failed miserably. Instead of sticking to downhill skiing, he decided to try a different approach at reaching his goal. Eddie didn't give up on his dream. He just came to the realization that making a slight tweak in his plan would possibly allow him to find better success. And he did.

Take it from Eddie—to be successful, you must change things about yourself that aren't allowing you to be successful. You can't cling to old habits and expect to magically become better. Change your attitude, your approach, your skillset, your career, and your lifestyle. Whatever it takes, don't be afraid of becoming a different person in order to reach your goals. It's pretty much mandatory.

Demand What You Want

Chances are, if you come from an unsuccessful family, you have been taught to just accept what is handed to you. Maybe things are unfair or unpleasant, but you just have to deal and survive. Right? WRONG!

There is a Muslim woman named Zaineb Abdullah. She is twenty-four years old and weighs 105 pounds, but she kicks butt and holds a black belt in karate. After her first experience being attacked by a racist man who grabbed the back of her hijab, she endeavored to teach self-defense classes for Muslim women in Chicago. This class isn't just about throwing punches, either. Abdullah says women in her classes are learning how to say "No!" and how to demand to be treated with respect. She encourages her students to prove that they are people too and to not just expect to be treated as humans, but to *demand it.* Since some say the Muslim culture teaches women to be more submissive and complacent, this class makes a huge impact on how these women view themselves. They are comfortable demanding what they want. As a result, they are standing up to sexual and racial violence.

Don't just accept what you are handed if it is not up to your standards. Instead, demand what you want. This ties in with fighting for what is right. You want to demand the best and accept only the best. Demand the life you want and the things you want.

When you demand things, people are more likely to give them to you. But when you demand things and refuse to settle for less, this action forces you to work for what you demand.

Don't Let Challenges Deter You

Every time Madonna tried to be successful, she faced a new challenge. She tried college, hated it, and dropped out. She tried to survive in New York City after that, only to be fired on her first day at Dunkin' Donuts when she squirted jelly all over a customer in line. Every direction she turned and everything she attempted, she faced a big challenge or a failure. Yet she didn't let that deter her from setting out to become a music icon and fashion diva. From the time she landed in NYC, she kept surmounting challenges to become the famous star we all know today.

You will not succeed unless you try, which means giving up is not an option. Instead of giving up, find ways to persevere.

Here are some common challenges:

Money

Time

People who don't believe in you or your vision

Social prejudice

Social limitations

Psychological issues

Health issues

Geographical limitations or transportation limitations (not having a car, living too far away from your dream school or dream job)

For each of these challenges, there is a solution. You just have to find it. That entails being bold and courageous, being creative and thinking outside of the box.

Raise the Bar

Let's compare two different types of people who've worked for me in my corporate America days. (The names have been changed to protect my wallet, of course.) The first, Michael, had super low standards. He didn't care about the work he put out because he knew he would get a paycheck for doing just the bare minimum. Michael was skipped over at every promotion cycle. Why would I promote someone who barely tried and didn't care about his quality of work?

Then there was Zane, a new hire. Zane expected perfection from himself so he worked really hard and produced top quality projects. Zane was someone whom I quickly promoted. Michael was mad because Zane was promoted before him, even though Michael had more seniority in the company. However, Michael failed to realize that Zane earned that promotion by proving himself and his work ethic time and time again.

Setting higher standards for yourself is the best way to make yourself go beyond your capacity and demand the best in life. You will never settle for less if you raise your standards.

So stop settling for second best. Make up your mind that you want something better. Then go after it. If you don't raise the bar, you will just fade away into status quo land like Michael, and you will offer no one anything that makes you valuable. Read that paragraph again. It's probably the most important one in this book.

When you raise the bar on yourself, you also expend more effort. When your hard work pays off, it's a huge confidence boost.

Nothing is more important to believing in yourself than having the confidence that you can do your best and succeed at everything you try. **How can you lose with an attitude like that?**

HOMEWORK TIME!

Refer to your *Not Afraid to Be First Workbook* to complete the **Chapter 4 exercise**.

CAST YOUR VISION

When businesses create a vision and missions statement, they tell the public what they hope to accomplish. They talk about how their work will help other people, which will ultimately help them reach their dreams of success.

You should want to do this for yourself. Define what your vision is and then think about how to achieve your vision through your dreams. Your vision should be like a huge net that you will cast with your dreams.

You can catch a lot of fish with the net. In other words, you can accomplish a lot when your vision, affects many people beyond just yourself.

Build Your Strategy on Your Vision

"Build your strategy from your stare." —TD Jakes

Bishop TD Jakes has so much advice about how to SOAR. In a memorable interview he gave to CBN News, he stated, "But if we don't balance inspiration with information, then it's going to lead to frustration." To achieve your vision and soar, you have to strike that balance. You can be inspired all day, but you have to find out how to make your vision happen. This is where a strategy comes in. Congrats to you for putting your strategy together with this book right now.

Stop Basing Your Vision on Others

Do you think you have a vision, but your heart isn't in it? Do you only hold onto this vision because others tell you that's what you should care about? Or, do you hold onto your vision because you want to make others happy? Maybe your mom wants you to do something that was really her dream. She lives it vicariously through you. Maybe everyone wants you to go to business school to make a lot of money, but business school plays no role in your real vision. You don't care about money as much as helping others. Well, when you base your vision on others, you miss out on doing what actually matters to you. What is in your heart is what gives you the passionate heat to carry your dream forward.

Your vision needs to be something you actually stand behind. It shouldn't be based on other people's opinions or their visions. Everyone can have a unique vision. Having a vision that is different from everyone else will not culminate into failure. In fact, it can make you succeed at being FIRST even more.

Plan It with a Pencil

It's time to start planning how you will manifest your goals. I call this section plan it with a pencil, because you need to do exactly that. While your ultimate goal needs to be in concrete, your plans are to be written in pencil, because they can and will change often. Writing your plans in pencil is also a psychological thing. If you go into your pursuit knowing that some things will go way better than you expected just as some attempts will appear to be futile, you will not be blindsided by any result. Regardless of the result, you must learn from them and make adjustments to your plans accordingly. Remember, this is a great thing. It's progress.

Back when I first learned how to DJ (little known Antonio Starr fact), my teacher, an Army soldier by the name of DJ Eboni out of Harlem, New York taught me the theory of "fixing it in the mix." I would have a record playing, and in my head, I knew exactly how I wanted to mix in the next record and how good it would sound. The only problem was sometimes I would have the next record playing either too fast or too slow. When I faded the new song in, the beats were not perfectly blended. I would get frustrated and just abandon the entire mix, but Eboni showed me the art of either slowing or speeding up the record to match the beats up on the fly. We fixed it in the mix while the audience was listening in.

Don't be afraid to make adjustments to your plan mid-execution family. Make your pencil's eraser your greatest tool, but the eraser should be used to correct new mistakes, not repeated ones. #Marinate

Draw Up a Vision Board

Like your dream board, your vision board should have your vision laid out in an appealing fashion so you like looking at it. Having a vision board helps you stay focused on your vision. It reminds you each day what you are working for and why all of this work is so worth it.

When you lose steam, just look at your vision board. It can fill you up with inspiration to keep pushing forward.

HOMEWORK TIME!

Refer to your *Not Afraid to Be First Workbook* to complete the Chapter 5 exercise.

THERE WILL BE CHALLENGES

There is no denying that you will face some challenges. Remember, no one said this would be easy. When you overcome these challenges and become the FIRST, your sense of reward will astound you.

For every challenge, there is a subsequent solution. You are able to overcome anything and everything if you set your mind to it.

The power to overcome the challenges you face is already within you. You just have to take care not to blot that power out with negativity. Don't give up before you give yourself a fighting chance.

Lack of Resources (It's a Fallacy)

You may not have everything you need to get started. The lack of resources can be a huge challenge. You have to find or create the resources you lack. Tough, yes. Impossible, no.

You probably don't have a huge college savings fund somewhere, and you don't have any rich relatives about to leave you massive inheritances. When it comes to making money for your dreams *and* making money to survive, finding a balance can seem nearly impossible.

But consider the movie, *The Pursuit of Happyness* (this time, one of Will Smith's better movies). Smith's character was a homeless single dad who had to spend a night in a subway bathroom while crying tears of frustration and terror. He had literally nothing…and so he went after the resources he needed to become a stockbroker. Notice I said he *went after* the resources he needed. He didn't wait for someone to find him at his lowest point in that bathroom. The fact that this movie was based on the true story of Mr. Chris Gardner should be even more inspiring, because it proves you can start with nothing and get everything you deserve if you want it bad enough. Remember this. You are never lacking resources. Resources and resourceful people are all around you. Even right now as you read this book. You just have to get up and go get it!

For educational expenses, there are scholarships, loans, and even first-generational college student programs (People champion the bravery of the first ones) to help you get through school. There are even AmeriCorps programs, where you work for scholarships while earning a small living stipend too. For capital, you need to approach investors and get someone excited about your idea to procure funding. For education and experience, just try to pick up classes, courses, and skills wherever and whenever you can. Community colleges are great resources for gaining skills, as are free online courses.

You can find what you need. You just have to look.

Toxic People

That blowhard aunt who says you are just a hooligan and your rapping can't amount to anything. That teacher who laughed when you talked about your dreams of going to Harvard. That ex (notice I said ex) who said you were too weak and undesirable to make it in life. Yes, all of those idiots! They are toxic, in case you didn't know that.

You will have a ton of negative people in your life. Their very mission will appear to be to tear you down and limit you. Maybe they do this to protect you. Maybe they do this because they are jealous. Maybe they will do this because they don't understand or approve of what you are trying to do. They may have never tried to be successful and they are bitter, or they accept the life they lead as the good life. They just don't get why you want to change.

Don't let these people breathe toxic fumes into your life and kill the seed of dreams you have planted in your heart. Believe me, they will try. You are not here to impress other people. You are here to create a life customized for you, by you. Detox regularly.

Lack of Relationships

Just about everything you get will come from someone else. This means you have to get people to want to give you things. In turn, you need to build good interpersonal relationships. If you lack what you need to launch your dreams, then you need to find a person who possesses what you need (aka a resource). The next art you need to learn is the art of ingratiating. This means you must get yourself in the good graces of the person of whom you need help from. How can you ingratiate them in exchange for what they can share with you? We all have something to offer to the world and the people in it. How can you inspire or even impress the person who inspires and impresses you?

Try to leave every job on good terms so you can get references and keep meaningful connections. Do your best to not burn bridges because you never know when you might need someone later.

Visit a few business networking events or trade shows. You would be surprised at the kinds of people you meet at these types of events. Be sure to get yourself out there and hand out business cards. Promote your business, brand, or your idea. Talk to people about what you might need. I can't count the number of times I've mentioned my needs to someone in a conversation, and they immediately introduced me to someone who could help me.

Never be afraid to start conversations with people in your county extension office or chamber of commerce. These offices are there to help support people who start businesses. They can give you tons of resources and insider tips if you just take the time to talk to these people.

I recommend brushing up on business etiquette. There are videos on YouTube that can teach you all about manners and how to behave in business settings. I also highly recommend a book called, *The Little Black Book of Connections* by Jeffrey Gitomer. This book taught me so much about business etiquette and no doubt saved me from ruining a lot of first impressions and more importantly, relationships. When you behave the right way and show respect, you can gain a lot of traction with the people you need to know.

For each person you meet, consider the value they can add to your life. What can they help you with? How can they help you reach your goals? Most importantly, evaluate how you can do the same for them. Keep your eyes peeled for potential business partners as well. Watch people for their business savvy and integrity. Don't forget to list your needed resources in your plans, so you will have a purpose for your networking while you're out there getting what you deserve.

Lack of Funds—Invest in Your Future

Any money you invest into your future is not a waste. It will certainly be useful later on. Use every day as a chance to build your future by investing in some small things that will later pay off. Remember me speaking about having a strategy? This area is where strategy will be crucial. Strategic spending is a must for you if your funds are low. In addition, you must be disciplined enough to know the difference between the things you want and the things your dreams need right now. Utilize your resources and your creativity to reduce out-of-pocket expenses.

I have saved thousands of dollars just by leveraging YouTube as an education platform as opposed to a prank watching source. I once learned Micro Economics for a CLEP test totally on YouTube. In lieu of buying a course, I learned how to set up and launch my First Generation Millionaire Clothing line entirely on YouTube. It's one of my greatest resources. There are so many ways you can creatively educate yourself on the internet alone. Just remember to stay focused on the main goal.

Do not get caught up in the "looking the part" syndrome that so many other derailed dreamers have. Now that you have a dream and vision board, you can likely touch, feel, and even taste your future. Stay disciplined though. Remember you are not investing in the present, but the future. There will be plenty of time for celebration after you cross the finish line.

Where there is no money, invest time and creativity. Where there is money, invest it strategically.

HOMEWORK TIME!

Refer to your _Not Afraid to Be First Workbook_ to complete the Chapter 6 exercise.

BECOME YOUR BEST SELF

You can't expect to soar into success as a FIRST if you are not performing at your best. Being your best enables you to give your fullest, grade-A effort to your dream. It enables you to make your dream come true using your own strength and willpower.

"You can only be fruitful if you are seedful."

This is another gem I received from Bishop TD Jakes. Identifying your seed is what causes you to become fruitful. So basically, you must find what you are good at and what you can offer the world.

Plus, your reputation is not something you should ever underestimate. To become successful, you must have valuable connections. No one will want to associate with you if you have a terrible reputation. Work on creating a great reputation that will precede you into your goals. It will make you so much more successful.

Strengthen Your Weaknesses

One of my old bosses back when I was a kid working in fast food liked to do everything in the establishment. The one thing he was not good at was customer service. He was downright rude, and we got complaints about him. A lot of employees were forced to do his duties as a manager by mitigating the damage after he pissed customers off. Had he realized his limitations, he might have earned fewer bad reviews for the restaurant. He could have also worked at becoming a bit more…customer friendly.

If you are struggling in any area of your life or your plan, then admit it to yourself right away. It's better that you're honest. You can avoid a lot of problems if you come clean about your limitations. Find someone who is good at what you are not and figure out how to create a win-win situation for them to help sharpen your skills, or better yet, do it for you. Don't allow your perceived weakness to be your absolute weakness because of foolish pride. Get help!

Listen to (some of) Your Critics

Here's the thing, in order to grow, you need to be open to the feedback of the people around you. The downside to being so determined to achieve a goal, vision, or dream is that we can sometimes get so deep into our zone that we can miss the minor details that shape our outcome. To remain grounded and properly aligned with your goals, you will need critics. Notice I said critics, not haters. Your true critics are the qualified people in your life who can speak without bias or vile intent on the things you are doing right as well as the areas that you may need to revisit. We call it constructive criticism, because the people who give it to you are ultimately trying to build you up, even if they are telling you to destroy a few things in your plan.

When a restaurant gets a bad review, the manager will usually contact the person to set things right and will coach the staff to ensure that the bad experience doesn't happen to more guests. When a writer submits their work to an editor, they get a ton of criticizing notes back telling them what they did wrong and how they can make the book better. When a teacher tells you your handwriting is not good and makes you practice it, you learn to write more legibly (my handwriting still sucks by the way). These are examples of when people use constructive criticism to actually build you up.

To receive constructive criticism effectively, you must remove all emotion from your mental receptors. If you are emotional at the time of criticism, you may mistake your trusted critic for a hater and stand a chance of missing valuable insight. Read that last sentence again!

Use Mentors, Coaches, and Role Models

You don't just enter the world knowing what to do. It would be nice if you had some sort of internal cellular knowledge for how to become FIRST, but life does not work that way. Since your family may have not prepared you to be successful, you need to find other people to teach you the ropes. A mentor or coach can do this for you. These people may work as life mentors or lifestyle coaches, or they may simply be people in the particular field you are getting into, or they may be career people, teachers, or tutors.

Always have a role model to look up to. These people provide tons of inspiration and motivation because they have accomplished what you hope to achieve. Some of my greatest coaches and mentors do not even know I exist and that's because they are my virtual mentors. A virtual mentor is that person who gives away most of their knowledge for free online. All because they believe in the gift of giving. By the way, most of my virtual mentors are right there on YouTube. I cling to every piece of content they share online. One day I will meet each of my VM's in person, so please be sure to tell everyone you know to buy this book, so they will know my name. LOL

Seriously. You do not have to live in a major metropolitan city or have well connected parents to be mentored by some of the greats in whatever area you are looking to conquer in life. I added that sentence in because I know some of you are still using the, "I don't know anyone" excuse as to why you can't go for it. Your mentors, coaches, and role models are out there waiting for you. Run to them!

You Are What You Speak

The way you talk and the things you say reflect on you. Consider a politician. If he or she has non-racist policies, but he runs around talking like a racist, you can assume he or she is a racist and that can influence your vote. Well, the same principle applies to you. People may not want to associate with you if you speak in insidious ways.

Try to avoid doing the following things that reflect badly upon you.

Gossiping

Speaking when you don't know all the facts

Talking trash about people you don't even know

Making rude or insulting statements

Using poor grammar (this makes you look uneducated and unintelligent)

Using slang that others can't understand

Using ethnic slurs or other racist terms

Making promises that you don't deliver

Bragging endlessly about yourself, revealing an over-inflated ego

Talking badly about yourself (people will believe what you say, and they will not always get self-deprecating humor)

Complaining about the homes, offices, actions, appearance, or work of others

Spouting political opinions in a non-political setting

Speculating about other people, especially when you don't know the truth

Getting very emotional and talking about how you feel a lot of the time

Getting aggressive and starting arguments with people, particularly over small things that don't matter

Lying

Telling grandiose and untrue stories for shock value and entertainment

Making inappropriate jokes

Smiling to someone's face and then talking smack about him or her as soon as he or she leaves the room

Believe it or not, these are only a few examples of many that take people out of their own game mentally. Regardless of what you face throughout your journey to be FIRST, you must speak greatness into yourself and everyone who you come in contact with, including your haters. Speak greatness into everyone! What you put out is what will come back to you almost every time.

Always Practice Integrity

I enlisted in the United States Air Force back in January of 1994. After completing Basic and Tech(nical) School training, I was given my first duty station in Oklahoma (I know that sounds crappy, but I requested to be there). One of the first things I was given as part of my in-processing procedures was what we called the *Air Force Core Values*. The very first thing I saw written in those core values was Integrity First.

Without your integrity, you will get nothing and nowhere of significance for a sustained amount of time. Regardless of what you are building, it will never stand upright if you are absent of uprightness within yourself. If you say you will do something, do it! If you did something, admit to it. Don't do something if you know it is wrong. Be honest, deliver on your promises, and keep your nose clean. Practicing integrity is a pretty basic concept. If no one knows you for anything else, you must make sure they are confident in your good character. Treating people with integrity will inspire confidence within them and within yourself. Word of mouth is a powerful thing so other people will learn about how great you are to work with before you ever meet them. Make sure of that!

Be Fast

To be at your best, you can't lag. You have to jump on opportunities before they disappear. You have to perform work in a timely manner and meet deadlines so people you work with can trust you. Finally, you have to take action before the chance to make a difference in your life passes by. And yes, the chance can and will pass you by if you allow it to.

Being fast does not mean to hurry and screw things up because you don't take your time. It means to seize life and live it to the fullest right away.

Get Yourself a Pacemaker

I know you read that and thought "a pacemaker? I thought he said this will be fun." Well, lucky for us, I'm not talking about the pacemaker that helps your heart function. I'm talking about the pacemakers that keep you on pace to achieving your goals. Earlier, I mentioned Sir Roger Bannister's team that helped him go beyond his capacity and make history. Well, the most important people on his team that day were his pacemakers. Their names were Chris Brasher and Chris Chataway. Their job was to give Bannister a visual marker of where he needed to be as far as time was concerned to break the record. In other words, his pacemakers were there to push him, but more importantly, they were there to prevent him from pushing too hard unnecessarily and causing burnout. Making history without failure was the goal.

You will need a pacemaker (some may call them rabbits) on your journey to success. Your pacemaker is simply someone who is currently on the path that you are traveling to meet your goal and making great strides (no pun intended). A pacemaker will let you know if you are falling behind, or if you are just doing too much at the moment. This journey of yours will be a marathon, so doing too much too fast is almost a surefire way to burning yourself out. Identify your rabbit and chase him/her! When the time comes to pass them up and lean into (sorry for all the racing analogies) your victory, you will know it.

Develop a Sense of Worthiness

How do you feel about yourself? When something good happens to you, do you think you don't deserve it or that you got lucky? Well, stop that! You must convince yourself you are worthy of all blessings that are bestowed upon you. You must believe in your worth. It will reflect in your work.

There is however, a huge difference between feeling worthy and feeling entitled. An entitled person feels they should win by default all because of who they are. The worthy person knows they have truly put in the blood, sweat, and tears and have worked with integrity, so when they do win, they deserve the celebration. Remember your affirmation statements. You are worthy!

Posture Up!

As we round out the traits and behaviors you must exhibit to become your best self, it all comes down to this. Posture! Posture has two meanings in the context of becoming FIRST. The first is your physical posture aka the way you carry yourself. People with lower self-esteem tend to display it in the way they carry themselves. Their shoulders are often slumped along with their head and eyes. Most people, especially the ones you will want in your inner circle can spot low self-esteem and unworthiness from a mile away. Conversely, extreme confidence is also worn in your physical posture, and it too will be felt as soon as you walk into a room.

At this point in the book, you are prepared to be a FIRST, so carry yourself as such at all times. Chest out, head high, swagger in your stride, firm handshake, and make eye contact with everyone you meet. That's the physical posture of someone who is supposed to be there!

The other posture you must display daily is all in your attitude and how you handle things in your life. I call this mental posture because it's all about the mental discipline one must possess to deal with people and situations you will face along the way. A person with mental posture looks at situations totally different than their weaker counterparts. A person who is postured up mentally doesn't allow problems to knock them off their pace. When you're postured up mentally, you focus on the resolution as opposed to the problem.

A postured-up person doesn't dwell on the proverbial mountain in front of them. Instead, they remain focused on the process(es) needed to scale that mountain. There is no time to complain, because all that does it delay your action. When you meet the right mentor, he or she will likely have very little time to dedicate to your complaints or excuses. They will be looking for posture and execution!

Lastly, the way you present your ideas to others will require all of your posture training. Not only do you have to present yourself physically postured up, but all the words that come out of your mouth must contain posture aka confidence. Posture yourself as being 100 percent confident in every word you utter. If you don't believe your own words, then don't expect anyone else to. Remember our discussion on critics? The opposite of emotion is posture, so when feedback and constructive criticism or anything else comes your way, posture up!

Create Your Avatar

When I first started my journey in online marketing, which included network marketing, I was all over the place trying to figure out how to get people to join me in business. I was talking to everyone who would listen to me. I didn't care if they had integrity, posture, or any traits I've tried to drill into your brain throughout this book. All I cared about was if they had the money to get started. That worked out terribly for me.

One of my mentors (#Message) told me I needed to sit down and take time to create an avatar of what my ideal business partner looked like. Up until that point, the only avatars I knew were those really tall blue people in the movie *Avatar*. An avatar, according to Dictionary.com, is "*an incarnation, embodiment, or manifestation of a person or idea,*" so that meant I needed to not only write out the traits of my avatar; but also paint a mental picture of him in my head, so when I saw him, I'd recognize him. Genius!

What I want you to do is take this information and create an avatar of your future self—this person you strive to be one day. Cast that image right now. List the qualities of your future self in your workbook, and make it as detailed as you can. This is different than your dream board and vision board, so don't try to skip out on this task.

What does your avatar look like on the day that your ultimate goal has been accomplished? What do the people look like who are closest to your avatar? What are they saying about your avatar when your avatar isn't around? How does your avatar feel about his or her accomplishments? Now go out and make that avatar the real you!

HOMEWORK TIME!

Refer to your *Not Afraid to Be First Workbook* to complete the Chapter 7 exercise.

KNOW WHEN TO QUIT

"Envision where you are going and then you can tell what you don't need."

—TD Jakes (again!)

Before flying international, you pack three bags of stuff you might need. Then you learn that your airline charges at least fifty dollars per checked bag. You can't afford $150 for your three bags, so you have to repack. This time, you have to be choosy and pack only the vital things you can't buy overseas.

This is the perfect metaphor for the baggage you carry through life. Do you have anything extra weighing you down, costing you money or resources that you don't really need? Could you save yourself some hassle by dropping a few bags? Learning who and what you don't need is essential to streamlining your life and thus bringing about success.

When Quitting is Good

So far, we have stressed the idea that you must never give up. Quitting on yourself is the surest way to kill your dream, but there are certain things you need to quit. This chapter is all about evaluating your life to find the things you don't need. These things stress you out and cause you to spread yourself too thin unnecessarily. They steal time, resources, and energy from your dreams. Dream Killers must go!

Quit Bad Habits

In the previous chapter, we talked about becoming your best self in order to become FIRST. While you don't need to become perfect, you do need to strive to be your very best. What is the number one habit that is keeping you from being your best self? Bad habits suck your creativity and productivity dry. They encourage you to do things that will ultimately hinder your success. These habits can and most often will hurt other people as well.

When we think about our bad habits, we tend to go straight to the worst-case scenarios that are drinking and drugs. While these probably are the worst-case scenarios, there are so many other bad habits that can kill everything you dream to accomplish. Procrastination is and will likely always be the number two killer of dreams around the world. Procrastination ruins timelines, and ruined timelines ruin execution, which in turn ruins relationships. I'd venture to say that a functioning alcoholic stands a better chance at success than a chronic procrastinator. That's mainly because I do not know any functioning procrastinators performing at the level of greatness. Remember integrity. Do what you say you will do in the time period you said you would do it.

Of course, there are many other bad habits that prevent us from greatness, which include but are not limited to:

Self-doubt

Habitually quitting too soon

Laziness

Resisting change

Resisting new environments

Being too emotional

Prejudging others

Isolating yourself

Having a short fuse

Poor eating habits

Lack of adequate rest (I added these last two as a reminder to myself)

How many of these bad habits are part of your daily routine? Here is what's good about addressing bad habits. The antithesis of each bad habit is very easy to identify. All it takes is for you to do the exact opposite of what your procrastinating self is doing daily. You know that you are prone to quitting endeavors at the first sign of a struggle. If you consciously decide to push past that urge to quit enough times, you'll find that quitting will begin to feel worse than the pain of the struggle. That's what you call reprogramming your subconscious mind.

Below, we will have you write out your own admitted bad habits and the antithesis to each of those habits. Writing this stuff out has a way of forcing you to address yourself with intention.

Identify Who to Quit in Your Life

Toxic people need to go! The people who are detrimental to your success will not add anything to your endeavors. In fact, they will drag you down like concrete blocks tied to your feet.

Watch what happens when you stop hanging out with toxic people or entertaining what they say. Your self-esteem skyrockets as you begin to believe in yourself instead of their negativity. Your sense of success soars as you begin to actually make an effort, because you believe you can do it. Your mood improves, because you no longer have people digging at your self-esteem, saying you won't amount to anything.

Here's how to tell if someone is toxic:

He/she never seems happy for you when you accomplish something.

He/she tells you that you can't do anything of significance.

He/she engages in chronic gossip.

He/she has debilitating bad habits like serious drug or alcohol use.

He/she makes you feel bad about yourself or what you are doing.

He/she is complacent in life.

He/she is extremely jealous.

He/she is inconsistent in their own life.

Your mood is lowered after hanging out with this person.

You have to hide who you are around this person to avoid criticism.

You feel defensive or threatened around this person.

You constantly have to explain yourself or apologize for your actions, even when you do nothing wrong.

A toxic person can be anyone—an old friend since kindergarten, a neighbor, a business partner, or a family member. Some of these toxic people may share a bed and kids with you, and that's where it gets tough because you likely still love them. What I'm about to say will not go over well with some people, but I have to give you my truth. If your spouse, mate, boyfriend, girlfriend is not equally yoked with you and your vision, then they must go. There is a saying, "I can do bad by myself" that I live by daily. I tell my wife (whom I am about to celebrate my twentieth wedding anniversary with at the time of this book's publishing) all the time that if she ever feels I am anything but her biggest cheerleader, then she needs to leave me, because I will do the same to her.

I know I said that procrastination is one of the biggest dream killers, but it's actually tied with toxic people who you allow in your life. Toxic people choose to be the way they are, so it is never your fault. A good, loving, and supportive person who is healthy for you will never tear you down or make you feel bad for doing well in life.

There is another thing that can make slashing these toxic people hard: You may worry that you will be all alone. But trust me, better friends and mates exist out there. You will meet more and more encouraging people as you climb up the mountain of success. Just like with toxic foods, once you cleanse your spirit of the toxic people, you will begin to glow, and that glow will attract people who love the light. Toxic people are intimidated by your glow.

Quit Endeavors that Don't Contribute to Your Success

Time is finite.

Manage it well by setting up a routine and setting aside time for your dreams and goals. It's important to have things you look forward to doing, and you need to enjoy your life even as you work on your dreams. Your dreams should not become a cage that trap you and don't give you time to have fun; but if you don't have enough time left to work on your dreams, then you, my friend, are having a prioritizing issue. You will also find that sometimes, you waste time doing things you don't really need to do at all. Imagine what you could do with the hours you spend binge-watching the next sci-fi TV show or reading up on what your favorite celebrity did on their extravagant vacation.

If it doesn't make progress, it doesn't make sense! This again is where you have to consciously reprogram your subconscious mind with your new success mindset. I remember one time I took a break from work to see what was happening on Instagram (follow me @antoniostarr) and ended up spending two hours watching one-minute video clips. Two hours! We have to quit all those time-wasting activities.

Here's a cheat code. Whenever you take a break from work, just set an alarm on your phone to pull you out of that sunken place of purposeless activities, so you do not overdo it.

Quit Being Impatient

Some parts of your plan will come together like a pallet of sod, meaning it will fall right into place, perfect with very little effort. Most of the time though, your plans will be more like spreading seeds in your yard and waiting for them to germinate and take root. It will take a long time for you to see the results of your plan in action. Most often, your plan will require cultivation of relationships and ideas, and for some people, this can become very discouraging. Patience is a virtue, my friend. If you've done everything you needed to do in the process, then time will do its part as long as you are patient enough.

Instant gratification is running rampant in our microwave society these days, but instant gratification doesn't typically lead to long-term greatness. We are here for long-term greatness, right? Quit being impatient!

By the way, even the sod requires consistent watering, attention, and patience. #Marinate

Be Not Afraid to Quit a Plan

While you should never give up on your ultimate goal, there will come times when you may have to give up on a plan. Remember earlier when I said to plan it with a pencil, so you can make adjustments? Well, some plans you will come up with will be better handled by ripping the entire piece of paper up. Most of these plans may come in the beginning stages once you start realizing you are including or excluding the wrong people and resources. This is to be expected in the beginning, so don't let it discourage you. A plan is a theory and assumptions, but often the assumptions are all positive and rarely err on the side of caution.

Have you ever heard of Sir Richard Branson? How about Virgin Records or Virgin Airlines? Does Virgin Cola ring a bell? Probably not as it was a plan and an actual product that Sir Richard brought to the market, but it didn't go as planned. Not even close! They had to pull the plug on the entire Virgin Cola plan with the quickness. Since most of us may not have billions of dollars in assets and investment capital, you have to be a bit more precautious in your planning. I'm not saying to plan scared; I'm telling you to plan smart, and do not be afraid to quit a plan if you see things are not going at all how you've planned. Sometimes, when you add a great resource to your team, a much smarter way to reach your goal becomes obvious. Keep a lot of paper and pencils close by.

HOMEWORK TIME!

Refer to your *Not Afraid to Be First Workbook* to complete the Chapter 8 exercise.

IF THEY DID IT, THEN SO CAN YOU

I added this chapter to the book just in case you still have a little bit of "You don't understand my issues, Antonio…" or the age old adage, "I still need to see it to believe it," and I totally get it.

This is why I want to introduce you to a few more people who are just like you and I. Some are minorities. Some come from humble beginnings, and some come from unthinkable conditions. The point is, if they did it, then so can you.

Success Rates of a Few Firsts You May Know

Have you ever heard of Jordan Peele? As I write this book, he just became the first black person to win an Oscar for Original Screenplay. That's major! In 2018, there are still so many FIRST's left to be conquered. In his acceptance speech, Mr. Peele stated, *"I stopped writing this movie about twenty times because I thought it was impossible. I thought it wasn't going to work."* He also said, *"I thought no one would ever make this movie. I kept coming back to it, because I knew if someone let me make this movie, people would hear it and people would see it."*

He never abandoned his ultimate goal, even though his plans likely changed with every stoppage he had in the writing process. Let this be a lesson that your fears are not necessary. Sure, you might fear failure and failure might happen! This does not mean you can't make a huge comeback. Just because you come from humble origins, or just because success is not yours at first, does not mean you will never be successful. Fight!

Let's look at a few other people who rose from rags to riches.

Richard Branson (Remember him? The guy with the failed cola company). He struggled with dyslexia and didn't do well at all in school. He started his first business in a church. Now he is valued at $4.6 billion, he's the fourth richest person in England.

J.K. Rowling. Did you know that the famous Harry Potter author started out as a struggling single mom who could barely afford the typewriter she wrote the first Harry Potter novel on? After writing the book, she experienced hundreds of rejections trying to get *Harry Potter and the Sorcerer's Stone* published. She battled suicidal tendencies and depression as well. Now she's a cultural icon who is richer than the Queen of England!

Daymond John. Once a black boy growing up in the "rough" section of Queens, New York, Daymond John started selling wool hats at half the market value. His mother voluntarily mortgaged her house to help him expand his vision and business (how's that for a resource?). Not only did he create an iconic fashion line, but he is now one of the most sought-after influencers in business in general.

Chris Gardner. This guy is the inspiration behind Will Smith's character in *The Pursuit of Happyness* that I mentioned earlier. He grew up in foster care and was a homeless single dad for a spell while raising his son. Then he became the CEO of the majorly successful stock brokerage Gardner Rich & Co.

I can go on and on with names and explanations, but you get the point, right? If not, here it is again. The above names or any other individuals mentioned in this book are no different than you or I when it comes to life's situations and issues. The only thing that separates these firsts from those who are last was a dream. A dream powered by a vision and an unwavering work ethic.

LASTLY

You are just one step closer to becoming FIRST in your family. Aren't you excited for when you can say, "I did it! I was scared out of my mind for a number of reasons, but I manifested my vision!"

Well, I hope and feel strongly that you are one day closer to becoming FIRST than you were before you began reading this book, but this book is far from the only step you have to take.

With each goal you complete on your list, and each step you take in your action plan, you get that much closer to your ultimate goal. Every day is a chance to work on making your dreams come true.

You can do it! You can become FIRST. It won't be easy, but it won't be as hard as you imagine. Each challenge will be worth it when you reach your end goal. The feeling of glory you will experience when you make your dreams come true will be the highest level of euphoria. First, you do have to make some changes. Learning to embrace change and take action toward those changes is crucial to making your life infinitely better.

Your dreams will never just magically come true. Someone is not going to come up to you and hand you your dreams on a silver platter despite what Television aka Tell Lie Vision may tell you. You have to work for it. But, that hard work just makes you love and appreciate your success as FIRST even more in the end. It will be worth it, trust me.

Surely you have some fears and some doubts. When these fears and doubts get so strong that you want to give up, just look at your avatar and your sources of motivation. Remember why you started doing this whole endeavor to be FIRST in the first place. That will give you the strength to overcome and banish these fears and move forward.

Instant gratification does not work when it comes to sustainable dreams and ultimate goals. Elbow grease is what makes dreams happen. So, you have to be patient. Work at your goals every day and watch success build upon itself.

There will be people in your life who tell you this isn't possible. They will tell you that you're wrong for even trying, or that you are ungrateful for the life you have been given, or that you think you are "better than everyone else." Don't listen to them. They never tried hard enough to be FIRST. Just because they don't encourage or support you does not mean you are wrong. You are more than right for wanting to better yourself and elevate your family. By the way, get rid of those people!

You will also run into hurdles. Plenty of hurdles. Remember that these are just part of life, and they are surmountable. You can achieve anything as long as you maintain the right attitude and keep trying. The only way to truly fail is to give up completely, so just persevere and watch your effort pay off.

Be sure to celebrate every small victory and every success. You deserve the applause! Even if you are the only person in your fan club right now, lavish yourself with loving encouragement to motivate yourself to continue moving forward. Each success, even the tiny ones, is one step closer to being FIRST.

This book is always here for you. Maybe you will need to look it over from time to time. Use it as a resource to support yourself and give yourself encouragement. You can use the workbook and redo your action plan whenever you need to. Staying on track is key, so be sure to gauge your progress and direct yourself as you need to.

So what are you waiting for? Your dream is entirely possible. You just have to make the first move, and those moves start right now!

CREATING YOUR ACTION PLAN!

Now you have gone through all the content in this book. How can you turn flat words on paper into something real that you can springboard your dreams off of? The answer is an action plan!

Using your answers to the homework questions in your workbook, you are going to formulate your plan. This plan will be your guide to the ACTIONS you need to take each day to reach your ultimate goal.

With your plan on paper, you will discover it's even more achievable than you previously thought. You just need to take the steps you outlined. Remember that everything happens on its own timeline. Some steps on your plan will take longer than others, but setting a deadline can inspire you to actually work at your dreams, instead of just thinking about them. Also remember, this is an ACTION plan, so in order for it to work, you must take action daily!

PLEASE PROCEED TO THE ACTION PLAN SECTION OF YOUR *NOT AFRAID TO BE FIRST* WORKBOOK.

ABOUT ANTONIO

Antonio Starr graduated at the bottom of his high school class and now he prides himself on "helping others get to the top of their potential." He has created "NOT AFRAID TO BE FIRST: How To Develop Fearless Vision, Disciplines and Traits Needed To Make Your Own History" as yet another contribution to pushing the envelope and the people forward.

He is a keynote speaker, coach, and consultant who specializes in working with students as well as working professionals looking to develop personally and professionally.

Antonio is an award-winning author, vlogger, and podcaster (First Generation Millionaire Podcast) whose content is read and shared by thousands globally.

Antonio lives in Atlanta, Georgia with his wife Erika and their two children.

www.antoniostarr.com

antonio@antoniostarr.com

You can check out my cool pictures and things

on my Instagram: @antoniostarr

If you are still a fan of Twitter I'm over there

from time to time as well: @antoniostarr

Let's talk business on LinkedIn:
linkedin.com/in/antoniostarr

Join my Not Afraid To Be First Facebook group:
antoniostarr.com/fbgroup

I NEED YOUR HELP

If I had to take a guess I would say that you've reached this page because you've either completed the book, or you just thumbed your way back here. If you in fact read this entire book then chances are that you found value in it.

If you in fact did get value from the hard work we put into the making of this manuscript, I just ask one favor of you. In today's world an Amazon review is universally recognized and viewed as the gospel. I would be forever grateful if you took just a few moments to write a raving review on this book and its contents.

Now, here is something else that we can do for each other.

If you feel that this book can bring value to your students, organization, colleagues, business partners, family members, etc... feel free to reach out to us about bulk orders. With bulk orders we can customize the cover or add other internal touches to future resonate with your brand.

Please email Benny at booking@antoniostarr.com to set up a time for us to discuss further.

GLOSSARY

Attitude – This is the approach you take to life and the way you look at things. A good attitude will carry you far while a bad one will lead to your ruin.

Avatar – This is the image of who you want to become. It may not be who you are yet, but it sets the groundwork for what you must work toward and achieve. It is a role model that you create yourself.

Audacity – Grit. Guts. This is the courage and the flat-out "I don't care" attitude that lets you tell people where to stick it when they try to bring you down. It is the daring and the confidence to go after your dreams without letting anyone hold you back.

Confidence – This is how you carry yourself. It is your attitude that you deserve the best and that you are worthy. It is the belief that you can do it, even when others tell you no.

Courage – Courage is the drive that fills your body and lends you extra strength. It makes you willing to overcome your fears and do what you want to do. Living life as a FIRST takes a lot of courage because you don't know what is up ahead in life, but you do it anyway to find out.

Dreams – Dreams are your lifeblood. They are your reason to get up in the morning. They are what you want to work toward in your life. You must never let your dreams die; rather, plant them like seeds and let them grow and fill your life.

Excuse – A reason for abandoning your dreams that makes sense. Usually preceded by the words, "I can't…"

Failure – Failure is not accomplishing your goals. The only way to truly fail is to give up.

Fear – This is that gut-wrenching, skin-crawling, dizzying emotion that makes you abandon your dreams. Usually fear is based on nothing, but it overwhelms you and terrifies you to the point of giving up. Learning to ignore and conquer fear is essential to becoming first.

First – You are a rockstar. You are the real MVP. You are striking out and trying to become the first person in your family to be successful. Like a pioneer or a trail blazer, you are making new paths and building your own life as you want it, not as you know it to be.

Goals – Goals shape your dreams. They are little steps you must complete in order to accomplish what you have set out to do with your life. They make

success possible while giving you something to work on.

History – Once you die, what memory do you want to leave behind? Do you want statues built for you in schools? Do you want foundations erected in your honor? Do you just want your kids to remember having a nice and safe childhood with financial stability? Well, that is the history you want to make. One day your future will be history and right now your future is yours to make, so work on making history.

Ingratiate – To get in good favor with someone through bringing value to them first.

Integrity – Doing the right thing, even when no one is watching. You do the right thing to do it, not to get a reward of some kind. You practice honesty and you are true to your word. You don't make empty promises, lie, cheat, or steal. When you don't deserve credit, you don't take it, and when you do wrong, you admit to it and pay the consequences.

Mentor – A wise teacher who can help you learn how to live life as a FIRST, and who can guide you since you have no family precedent to follow. They offer wisdom, stability, and security when you are uncertain how to proceed with being successful.

Might – This is a vague term that means you won't really do something. You can say that you might all day, but do you really do it? Might is full of weakness. Don't say "I might," say "I will."

Motivation – This is the drive to do something, even if there are challenges in the way. You gain motivation from people who love you or goals that you set or visions that you hope to one day cast over the world. Motivation pushes you through the tough times. Therefore, it is very important to have.

Role Model – This is a person to look up to, someone who has already done what you are setting out to do. Role models are living proof that what you dream of is possible. Their actions and lives inspire you and encourage you to go forward. You aspire to act more like them and achieve what they have.

Toxic – These are the people who discourage you, hold you back, or otherwise poison your dream. They are harmful people who are not helping you get ahead. They need to go.

Vision – This is how you see yourself impacting and changing the world. It is how you want your legacy to be remembered. Your goals and dreams come together to help shape your vision.

.